Color Me...CHERRY & WHITE

TEMPLE UNIVERSITY PRESS
Philadelphia, Pennsylvania 19122
tupress.temple.edu

Published 2018

Printed in the United States of America

ISBN 978-1-4399-1858-6

9 8 7 6 5 4 3 2 1

Color Me...
CHERRY & WHITE

A TEMPLE UNIVERSITY COLORING BOOK

T

TEMPLE UNIVERSITY PRESS
PHILADELPHIA • ROME • TOKYO

Russell H. Conwell, Founder of Temple University

Owl Stained Glass

Temple University SEPTA Regional Rail Station

Men's Basketball

Women's Basketball

The Bell Tower

The Bell Tower, one of the gifts from the Samuel Paley Foundation, is a freestanding bell tower set within a plaza in front of Paley Library. It is said to have a collection of rocks from Pakistan encased under the glass of the tower—Pakistan being one of the places of origin of the "Acres of Diamonds" legend. The Bell Tower is a popular meeting place for pep rallies and other student events. In warm weather, students gather on lawns known as Beury Beach to sunbathe, play Frisbee and other games, and study.

Food Truck on 13th Street

North Philadelphia

Men's Crew Team

Stained Glass Trio

Temple University Football Helmet

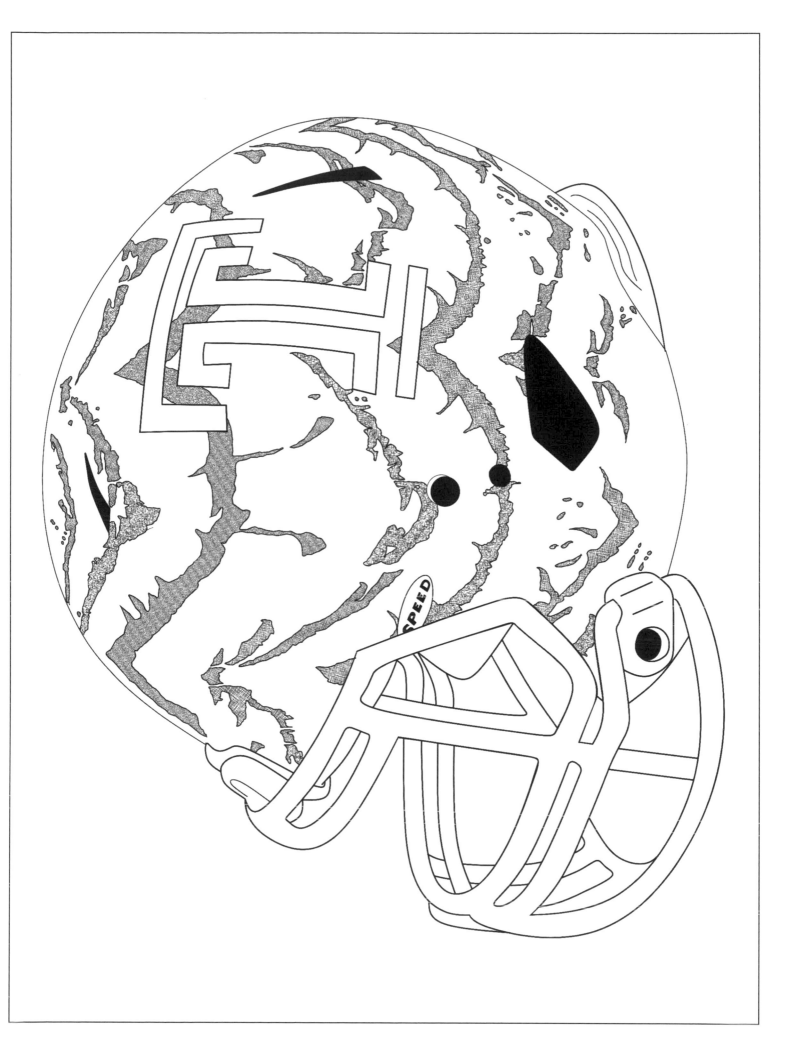

Baptist Church Stained Glass

The Baptist Temple (aka The Temple and Grace Baptist Temple) was opened on March 2, 1891 to much fanfare and was considered an architectural marvel of its time. The building's exterior is an example of the Romanesque Revival style in America with its most prominent feature a stained-glass half-rose window, 30 feet in diameter.

Temple University Seal in Stained Glass

Fencing Team

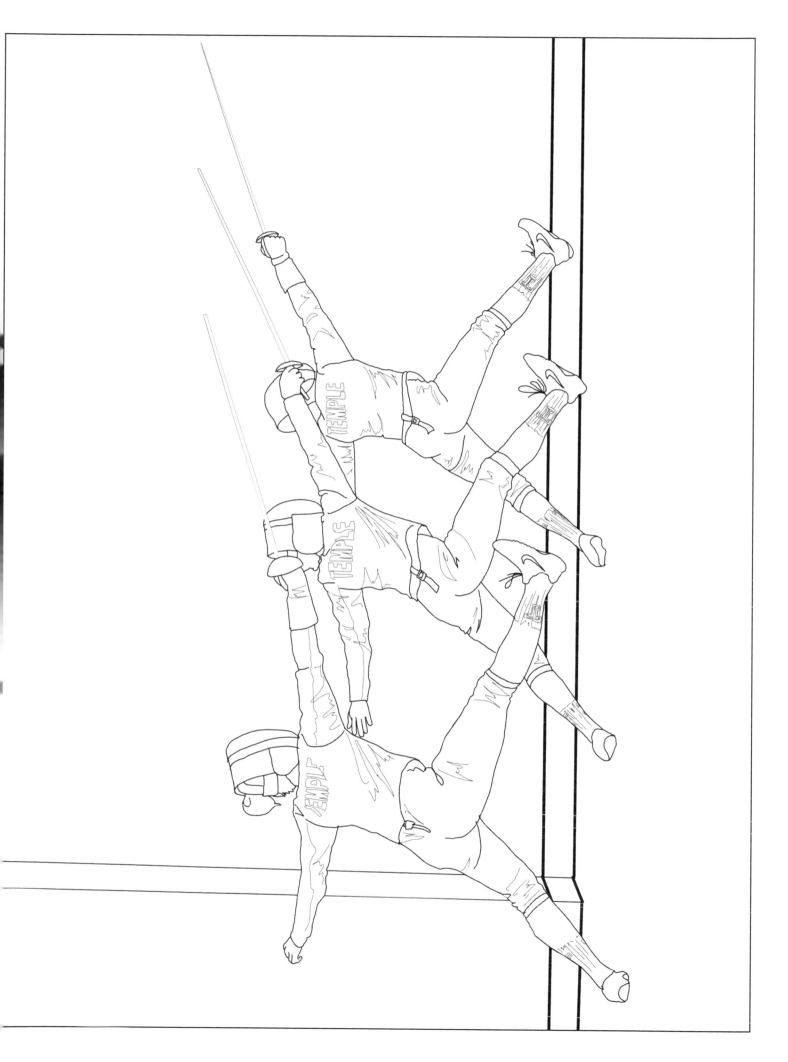

Temple University Seal on Campus Gate

Temple Mascot, Hooter

Howard Gittis Student Activities Center

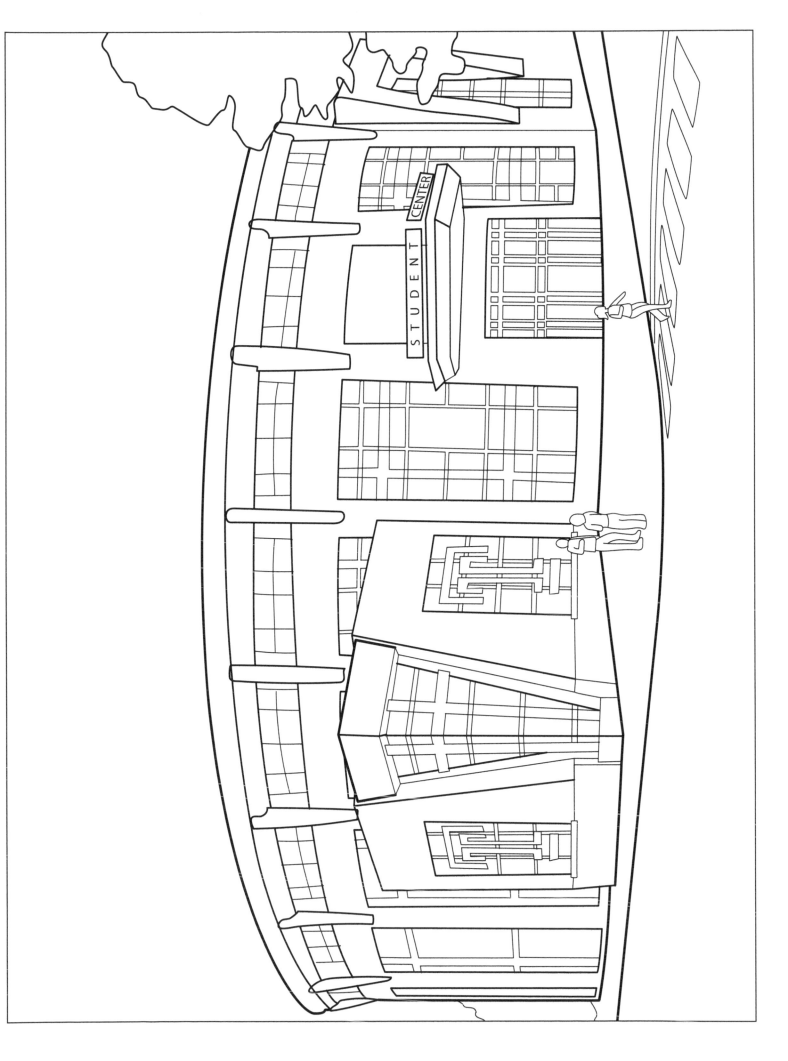

Alumni Circle

The Red Owl is mounted on top of the Alumni Circle, a stone seating area and gathering place along Liacouras Walk. The 3,000-pound sculpture of the head of an owl was created by an Italian artist and donated to Temple by Bell Atlantic in 1988.

North Broad Street

Safety Officers

Stella, the Temple Owl

Sullivan Hall

Paley Library Gardener